STRANGE FIRE, AUTHENTIC FIRE

JOHN KENNEDY BROWN

authorHOUSE

AuthorHouse™
1663 Liberty Drive
Bloomington, IN 47403
www.authorhouse.com
Phone: 833-262-8899

Published by AuthorHouse 02/23/2023

ISBN: 979-8-8230-0154-0 (sc)
ISBN: 979-8-8230-0153-3 (e)

Print information available on the last page.

This book is printed on acid-free paper.

CONTENTS

"DON'T THROW THE BABY OUT WITH THE BATH WATER"

In life there is yes and no, up, and down, in and out. There is near and far, before and after. There is positive and negative, wrong, and right. Also, there is the existence of a rage and a calm, a lie and the truth, there is God and the devil. Thus, none of these situations occur at the same time. I was walking down the street one day, an older sister in the Lord called me to the side and said, "do you know what your problem is?". She said, you believe everyone is real. She made a correct observation of me. I never tried to be judgmental, I just took a person's word about a matter. I had no reason to think any other way. I feel, there are two groups of people, those who think everyone is false and the other think that everyone is real.

I knew this woman who thought that everyone she met was not right. They were evil or she could see demons hanging from them. This person loved to start confusion. It seems she was the only person that was "always" correct. I also knew of this guy who was very critical of everyone, and no one was right in his eyes. He would sow discord among the people and in his twisted thinking, he felt that he was right.

This drives me to ask the question, are there false brothers and prophets? Of course, 2 Corinthians 11:26 states: *In journeys often, in perils of waters, in perils of robbers, in perils by mine own countrymen, in perils by the heathen, in perils in the wilderness, in perils in the sea, in perils among false brethren.* Galatians 2:4 provides further declares: *An that because of false brethren unawares brought in, who came in privily to spy out liberty which we have in Christ Jesus, that they might bring us into bondage.* Jesus said in Matthew 24:11 *And many false prophets shall rise and shall deceive many. So, is everyone false? Of course not,* Matthew 23:37 *"O Jerusalem, Jerusalem' you who kill the prophets and stone those sent to you. I have longed to gather your children together, as a hen gathers her chicks under her wings, but you were not willing."* The bible speaks of five ministerial gifts found in Ephesians 4:11 *And he gave some apostles; and some prophets; and some evangelists; and some pastors and teachers; prophets are named as one of those office gifts.* 1Thessalonians 5:19-21 *Quench not the Spirit, despise not prophesying, prove all things and hold fast to that which is good. If everything was false, you wouldn't have to prove anything against it.*

In other words, if a person gave you one hundred dollars, fifty of them was real and the other fifty was fake, would you throw them all away? Most people would find a way to distinguish between the two. Some people use money markers to determine the authenticity of currency. We must learn what the Word of God says on different subjects when we are confronted with them. We will have a better biblical view on them. Sola scriptura (Latin: by scripture alone) is a theological doctrine held by some Christian denominations that the Christians scriptures are the sole infallible rule of faith and patience.

Strange fire is a movement that appears to be from God, but it is not authorized by Him. Individuals must be careful about offering up things to God that He is not in. Hoping that He will honor their flesh or emotions because they are doing things in His name. *Leviticus 10:1-2 And Nadab and Abihu, the sons of Aaron, took either of them his censer, and put fire therein, and put incense thereon, and offered strange fire before the Lord, which He commanded them not. And there went out fire from the Lord, and devoured them, and they died before the Lord. Proverb 16:25 There is a way that seemeth right unto a man, but the end thereof are the ways of death.*

When it comes to most Pentecostals, Charismatic, Church of God in Christ and Non-denominations are very noisy people when it comes to Praising Yahweh (The Creator). Hallelujah is the Hebrew word meaning "Praise ye, Yah", translated using Hebrew's plural imperative form of you (in English being "ye") and the shortened form of Yahweh in Hebrew "Yah" (Praise you, Yahweh"). One of the Hebrew words for praise is halal, haw-lal' to be clear (orig. of sound, but usually of color); to shine; hence, to make a show, to boast; and thus, to be (clamorously) foolish; to rave; caus. To celebrate; also, to stultify.

Psalms 35:18 I will give thee thanks in the great congregation: I will praise thee among many people. Psalms 150:1-6 Praise ye the LORD. Praise God in his sanctuary: Praise him in the firmament of his power. Praise him for his mighty acts: praise him according to his excellent greatness. Praise him with the sound of the trumpet: praise him with psaltery and harp. Praise him with the timbrel and dance: praise him with stringed instruments and organs. Praise him upon the loud cymbals. Let everything that hath breath praise the LORD. Praise ye the LORD!

Many people go to sporting events where they want to see their team win. Spectators get verbally involved with hollering to the top of their voice on Saturday nights. Come Sunday morning service, some become quiet as a mouse. Why is this so? Fear may be involved. *2*

Timothy 1:7 For God hath not given us a spirit of fear; but of power, and of love, and of a sound mind. Sometimes we may have been taught not to believe what the Word of God says. I had two brothers in the Lord to tell me on different occasions that they didn't believe God to heal people; because their pastors didn't believe God could supernaturally heal people. Certainly, I am not against doctors and medical science, I thank Yahweh for them. Sure, there were praise and healing in the Hebrew scriptures which were realities. The words were also types and shadows that pointed us to the ultimate reality Yeshua (Jesus). Some people take strength from the Word of God and don't realize they are doing it. Jesus has not changed, nor his anointing *Hebrew 13:8 Jesus Christ the same yesterday, today, and forever.* The nature of Jesus, his words, principles, and characteristics are in unison with him. Those things of him can't be divided. Someone might not like it, but the truth remains.

Aaron entered a strange fire with the people against God. *Exodus 32:1-7 And when the people saw that Moses delayed to come down out of the mount, the people gathered themselves together unto Aaron, and said unto him, Up, make us mighty ones, which shall go before us; for as for this Moses, the man who brought us up out of the land of Egypt, we wot not what is become of him. And Aaron said unto them, break off the golden earrings, which are in the ears of your wives, of your sons, and of your daughters, and bring them unto me. And all the people brake off the golden earrings which were in their ears and brought them unto Aaron. And he received them at his hand, and fashioned it with a graving tool, after he made it a molten calf: and they said, these be the mighty ones, O Israel, which brought thee out of the land of Egypt. And when Aaron saw it, he built an altar (a place of fire) before it; and Aaron made a proclamation, and said, tomorrow is a feast to the Lord. And they rose up early on the morrow and offered burnt offerings and brought offerings;(strange fire) and the people sat down to eat and to drink and rose up to play. And the Lord said unto Moses, Go, get thee down; for thy people, which thou broughtest out of the land of Egypt, have corrupted themselves.*

If we are not careful, it is possible to get caught up in doing things in the name of God or Jesus. While it can be a ritual, click or performance and we may think it is spiritual. The Father dealt with me about the proclamation that Aaron made to him in the wilderness. It was a question, but it sounded more like a statement with strength. God said, how can you offer me something, when I am not in it? The answer is very simple, "you cannot". God said, people do things in his name to justify their means. This still happens today, some individuals think that if they use the name of God, they will have more strength within themselves, and over other people lives. We must study the Word of God for ourselves and stay prayerful, so that we can be sensitive to the Holy Spirit that lives in us. God stills speaks to and through his servants today! Why should He change? *Malachi 3:6 For I am the Lord, I change not; that ye sons of Jacob are not consumed.*

We can't put God in our box because He won't fit. Our denominations and intelligence are too small for Him. I have heard people say that God doesn't move in this way or that way, but I found the best answers are in the Word of God. One should always see what the scriptures have to say about the matter. When we do, we shouldn't allow pride to hold us in bondage to our traditions because we don't want to be wrong. In the word *states 1 Corinthians 2:16 For who hath known the mind of God, that he may instruct him? But we have the mind of Christ.* The bible lets us know that we have the mind of Christ but never to instruct him. Yahweh thoughts are much richer and profound than ours by far, simply He does not think the way we do. *Isaiah 55: 8-9 For my thoughts are not your thoughts, neither are your ways my ways, saith the Lord. For as the heavens are higher than the earth, so are my ways higher than your ways, and my thoughts than your thoughts.*

Some people take the scriptures and their mentalities to fight against God. They may be unaware in some cases. My personal experience with *Matthew 6:33 But seek ye first the kingdom of God, and his righteousness; and all these things shall be added unto you.* I used to write poetry and lyrics for songs, yet I was very impatient. I wanted to get them published, like yesterday. I remember talking to my mother about getting them published, she told me to have patience. When she did, the spirit of impatience rose up in my belly with heat. I really didn't want to hear about waiting on anything. Another thing, I didn't want to give God the glory for my success. I wanted it to be said, that I did it by myself. One day God showed me His kingdom slanted, I said, half-jokingly umm umm I gotcha. I knew it was more to the story than what I was perceiving. He said, it is not my kingdom that is slanted, it is you and when you start bending that is when things will start lining up.

CHAPTER TWO

THE SOURCE OF THE MANIFESTATION

There was a church service one night some people had invited others to come. They said signs and miracles would be happening at this place. They also told the individuals not to judge anything by the Word. They were told to flow with whatever occurred. Going with the flow would be a red flag and not too many would attend that service. One night a guy threw the bible on the floor and said I don't need this book I am filled with the Holy Spirit. Remember, the Spirit of God is never going to act apart from the Word of God. The Word of God is never going to act apart from the Spirit of God. They are in unison with each other, and they "always" agree. The Word of God is our foundation that we stand on.

Many years ago, I thought every supernatural occurrence was from the Spirit of God. I think many new believers are eager to see the power of the demonstration of the Holy Spirit. *1 Corinthians 2:4-5 And my speech and my preaching was not with enticing words of man's wisdom, but in demonstration of the spirit and power: That your faith should not stand in the wisdom of men, but in the power of God.*

Also, every supernatural event that occurs doesn't come from the devil. We must remember, we can't throw out the baby with the bath water. If some have hardened themselves against the Spirit of God and his servants concerning the miraculous, they can become very bitter and start fighting against the supernatural power of God. I was watching television one night and I saw a guy in a wheelchair talking. He said his friend invited him to a service. He also told him that God was going to heal him that night. So, he went expecting to be healed. He was prayed for, and nothing happened. His friend meant well by asking him to go to service. I would have told someone that they would be healed also expecting God to do so by faith.

But now that I think about it, I would have worded it differently. I would have worded it as such "Let's go to service tonight I am believing with you that God will heal you." Certainly, I would not have guaranteed him that he was going to be healed. Unless I had a sure word from God without a doubt. Obviously, the guy in the wheelchair believed that God was going to heal him but when he wasn't he got angry with the Father. He also resented all that called themselves faith healers whether they were real or not it didn't matter. Now, he must prove to the world that God does not heal. Now these men and women are charlatans, and they must be exposed.

This person was a believer in healing at one point. Continuationism to Cessationism Continuationism is a Christian theological belief that the gifts of the present age, specifically those sometimes called "sign gifts", such as tongues and prophecy are still active. Cessationism is the doctrine that spiritual gifts such as speaking in tongues, prophecy and healing ceased with the apostolic age. Some cessationist feel like God can only perform a miracle to prove a point. When God doesn't heal you, I used to hear about men of God that would pray for others to be healed and many would be.

Some minister prayed for healing for themselves but would

remain sick. That was a puzzle to me because I thought if God is healing through them why aren't they being healed. Back then I didn't think that if they had faith for others why wouldn't they have faith for themselves. Some things aren't so clear. In *Deuteronomy 29:29 The secret things belong unto the LORD our God: but those things which are revealed belong unto us and to our children forever, that we may do all the words of this law.* God has anointed us for others. I am not saying that we cannot partake of that anointing. The Father wants us to minister life to others. *Matthew 10:1 And when he called unto him his twelve disciples, he gave them power against unclean spirits, to cast them out, and to heal all manner of disease. Isaiah 61:1-3 The Spirit of the Lord GOD is upon me to preach good tidings unto the meek; he hath sent me to bind up the brokenhearted, to proclaim liberty to the captives, and the opening of the prison to them that are bound; To proclaim the acceptable year of the LORD, and the day of vengeance of our God: to comfort all that mourn; To appoint unto them that mourn in Zion, to give unto them beauty for ashes, the oil of joy for mourning, the garment of praise for the spirit of heaviness; that they might be called trees of righteousness, the planting of the Lord, that he might be glorified.*

One minister said that he believes the Holy Spirit is still moving and illuminating the Word. He also believes the Holy Spirit is still building the church up and He is part of our redemption. This pastor is highly recognized and has greatly influence the body of Jesus Christ nationally and internationally. He makes mention of the Holy Spirit but has place limitations on Him unaware. He and many others don't believe that the Holy Spirit is a person and he can speak or inspire someone to share information with others. God Almighty wants all His children to know Him personally. Jesus told his disciples He would send them another Comforter. *John 14:16-18 And I will pray the Father, and he shall give you another Comforter, that he may abide with you forever; Even the Spirit of truth; whom the world cannot receive, because it seeth him not, neither knoweth him: but ye know him; for he dwelleth with you and shall be in you.* In John 10 it says that Jesus sheep knows his voice.

The Holy Spirit is not a bird, water, wind, fire, or goosebumps. He is a person. The Holy Spirit, He, is also known as the promise. *Acts 2:38-39 Then Peter said unto them, Repent, and be baptized every one of you in the name of Jesus Christ for the remission of sins, and ye shall receive the gift of the Holy Spirit. For the promise is unto you, and to your children, and to all that are afar off, even as many as the Lord has call.*

If you ask for the Holy Spirit Luke *11:11-13 If a son shall ask bread of any of you that is a father, will he give him a stone? Or if he asks a fish, will he for a fish give him a serpent? Or if he shall ask an egg, will he offer him a scorpion? If ye then, being evil, know how to give good gifts unto your children: how much more shall your heavenly Father give the Holy Spirit to them that ask him?* Holy Spirit in the Greek is Paraclete He is your advocate, helper, standby, guide, counselor, strengthen and intercessor. The Holy Spirit brings things to your remembrance, and He is a teacher. *John 14:26 But the Comforter, which is the Holy Spirit, whom the Father will send in my name, he shall teach you all things, and bring all things to your remembrance, whatsoever I have said unto you.*

The person of the Holy Spirit in you is your guide and He reveals thing to come. *John 16:13 Howbeit when he, the Spirit of truth, is come, he will guide you into all truth for he shall not speak of himself; but whatsoever he shall hear, that shall he speak, and he will show you things to come.* Have you ever seen a three-dollar bill or a six-dollar bill? It is a good chance you won't. Hardly is there a fake made of anything if the original does not exist. Simon the sorcerer from being false to becoming real. *Acts 8; 9-14 But there was a certain man, called Simon, which before time in the same city used sorcery, and bewitched the people of Samaria, giving out that himself was some great one: To whom they all gave heed, from the least to the greatest, saying, this man is the great power of God. And to him they had regard, because that of long time he had bewitched them with sorceries. But when they believed Philip preaching the things concerning the kingdom of God, and the name of Jesus Christ, they were baptized, both men and women. Then Simon himself believed also: and when he was baptized, he continued with Philip, and wondered, beholding the miracles and signs which were done.*

Simon the sorcerer had used bewitchment to deceive the people as thou he was from God. He displayed an imagine of God without having the true substance of God which is Jesus. Simon walked in falsehood until he embraces the preaching of the kingdom of God and the name of Jesus Christ. There was a reality of the gospel of Jesus Christ that was more powerful than any magic that Simon could ever conjure up. The signs and miracles also got Simon attention. Many years ago, I used to be around a certain group of people, and from time to time I would say. It is just as easy to be real then it is to pretend. That only makes sense if you really look at it. Yahweh would show me a bowl of fruit but there was something to it it wasn't real. He was letting me know those folks was not genuine but initially I didn't comprehend what He was saying.

At times God is speaking to us and we don't know it. It is good to stay in the Word of God and ask the Father in Jesus name that you become more familiar with His Spirit. Psalms 103:7 God made known his ways to Moses and his acts to the children of Israel. If something violates the Word of God, it is not from God and if it pulls you from Him, it is not from God. *Deuteronomy 13:1-3 If there arise among you a prophet, or a dreamer of dreams, and giveth thee a sign or a wonder, And the sign or the wonder come to pass, whereof he spake unto thee, saying, Lets us go after others gods which thou hast not known, and let us serve them: Thou shalt not hearken unto the words of that prophet, or that dreamer of dreams: for God proveth you, to know whether ye love God your Lord with all your heart and with all your soul.*

Galatians 1:6-9 I marvel that ye are so soon removed from him that called you into the grace of Christ unto another good news: Which is not another; but there be some that trouble you and would pervert the good news of Christ. But thou we, or an angel from heaven, preach any other good news of Christ. As we said before, so say I now again, if any man preaches any other good news unto you than that which we have preached unto you, let him be accursed. Visionary ministry tells us that if you are sick and you have been praying for your healing, and someone walks in your room with a white robe on. This person has piercing near their wrist and have a crown of thorns on his head. Then he tells you it is not mine will for you to be heal. That is another gospel because *3 John 1:2 Beloved, I wish above all things that thou mayest prosper and be in health, even as thy soul prospereth.* If someone tells you to be fearful in life that isn't correct now there are things, we should be cautious of *2 Timothy 1:7 For God hath not given us a spirit of fear; but of power, and of love, and of a sound mind. The Spirit of the Lord today is moving in many sanctuaries. 2Corinthians 3:17 Now the Lord is that Spirit: and where the Spirit of the Lord is there is liberty. Mishkan- Tabernacle was a portable sanctuary, a spiritual center in the midst of the desert. Exodus 25:8 And let them make me a sanctuary; that I may dwell among them. 2Chronicles 5:14 So that the priests could not stand to minister by reason of the cloud: for the glory of the LORD had filled the house of God. Psalms 63:2 To see thy power and thy glory, so as I have seen thee in the sanctuary. Psalms 134:2 Lift up your hands in the sanctuary and bless God. Psalms 100:1-2 Make a joyful noise unto God all ye lands. Serve God with gladness: come before his presence with singing. This is what Jesus said in Matthew 18:20*

For where two or three are gathered together in my name, there am I in the midst of them.

If it is a few or many gathered together in Jesus name know that He is there. We can't determine with our natural mind what is the moving of the Holy Spirit. Of course, if you are optimistic concerning the Spirit of God you might want every manifestation to be from Him. Sometime people excitement or flesh can be acting out in Jesus name and He is not there. So, every occurrence will not be from God no matter how much you want it to be. If you have a pessimistic mentality about the Spirit of God never moves through people. There is a problem here also because you have built up barriers and walls in your mind, that when there is an authentic move of the Holy Spirit. You will automatically reject it because of your belief system. Thus, the optimistic and the pessimistic will teach from his theory but more importantly what does the Word of God says without your emotions being involved. *1Corinthians 2:10-16 But God hath revealed them unto us by his Spirit: for the Spirit searcheth all things, yea, the deep things of God. For what man knoweth the things of a man, save the spirit of man which is in him? Even so the things of God knoweth no man, but the Spirit of God. Now we have received, not the spirit of the world, but the Spirit which is of God; that we might know the things that are freely given to us of God. Which things also we speak, not in the words which man's wisdom teacheth; comparing spiritual things with spiritual. But the natural man receiveth not the things of the Spirit of God for they are foolishness unto him: neither can he know them, because they are spiritually discerned. But he that judgeth all things, yet he himself is judged of no man. For who hath known the mind of God that he may instruct him? But we have the mind of Christ.*

The Word of God always helps develop us. *Hebrews 5:13-14 For everyone that useth milk is unskillful in the word of righteousness: for he is a babe. But strong meat belongeth to them that are of full age, even those who by reason of use have their senses exercised to discern both good and evil.* Manifestations are seen all the time, but what is truly causing the obvious to appear God or the devil or someone emotions?

Source is inception, root mean the point at which something begins its course or existence. Origin applies to the things or persons which something is ultimately derived and often to the causes operating before the thing itself comes into being. Manifestation is a secondary response from its originality that produces the obvious. An unseen apple seed in the ground is a source that produces a tree that is a manifestation. So, by finding out the true source of a thing will help you know what is manifested. If you want to learn about plants by studying them wouldn't be a bad idea. If you study the seed, you will learn of the creativity of the plant before it is manifested. By studying the seed, you step into the future of that plant even thou you are still in the present.

When you equipped yourself in the now with the Word of God you are in your strategy room. That will help you in the future which is the battlefield. No soldier should never go to war without preparation and no professional should be without his library. I thank Yahweh that he has given us His bible that is filled with instructions and when you get the instruction you can start construction. I remember one night leaving Newellton, Louisiana heading home it was ice on the road. We started looking for the hazardous light switch near the steering wheel it couldn't be found. The Holy Spirit prompted me to get the manual out the glove compartment I obeyed Him thirty seconds later I found the hazardous switch it was near the radio. God Word will prompt you because it is alive anything that conveys a message has a voice. Thou it might not always be verbal it still speaks. Hebrew 4:12 For the word of God is quick and powerful, and sharper than any two-edge sword, piercing even to the dividing asunder of soul and spirit, and of joints and marrow, and is a discerner of the thoughts and intents of the heart.

2 Timothy 3:16-17 All scriptures is given by inspiration of God, and is profitable for doctrine, for reproof, for correction, for instruction in righteousness: That the man of God may be perfect, thoroughly furnished unto all good works. Has there been abuse and extreme measures done in the body of Christ? We know the answer is yes, I doubt it very seriously that Jesus ever commanded his disciples to bark like dogs. Nor did He tell his disciples to act like animals, at some meeting people want to be seen. Other people feel like this is what is expected of me to perform so they do it.

Some people don't won't the other person to outdo them, so they carry and put on. A minister told me another preacher was preaching at a rally and before he sat down. He looked a preacher in the face and said let me see you out do that. Does that mean that every preacher is doing an act or performance? No How about when people are having praise and worship is everyone trying to be seen? In every profession there is abuse or misuse is everybody in that field corrupted? No An authentic fire from heaven Elijah calls fire down. 1King 18:30-38 And Elijah said unto all the people, Come near unto me. And all the people came near unto him. And he repaired the altar of God that was broken down. And Elijah took twelve stones according to the number of the tribes of the sons of Jacob, unto whom the word of God came, saying, Israel shall be thy name:

And with the stones he built an altar in the name of God: and he made a trench about the altar, as great as would contain two measures of seed. And he put the wood in order, and cut the bullock in pieces, and laid him on the wood, and said, fill four barrels with water, and pour it on the burnt sacrifice, and on the wood. And he said, do it the second time. And he said, do it the third time. And they did it the third time. And the water ran round about the altar; and he filled the trench also with water, And it came to pass at the time of the offering of the evening sacrifice, that Elijah the prophet came near, and said, God of Abraham, Isaac, and of Israel, let it be known this day that thou art God in Israel, and that I am thy servant, and that I have done all these things at thy word. Hear me, O God, hear me, that this people may know that thou art God and that thou hast turned their heart back again. Then the fire of God fell, and consumed the burnt sacrifice, and the wood, and the stones, and the dust, and licked up the water that was in the trench. When a minister does not allow the Spirit of God to move in service, he does harm to the people. He will give in account of that, quenching the Spirit of God. I have seen some leaders that don't believe certain things that the bible says. If the pastor doesn't believe they are going to teach their members not to believe what the scriptures says. That's why it is important to study the Word of God for yourself. 2Timothy 2:15 Study to shew thyself approved unto God, a workman that needeth not to be ashamed, rightly dividing the word of truth. Let the real God become personal in your life.

God has always been real, but some have not made Him personal in their lives. I want to share this example with you before you purchase your cell phone it was real, but it was not personal to you. But when you purchase your cell phone and took it home and activated it and start using it it became personal to you. Hebrew 4:2 For unto us was the good news preached as well as unto them: but the word preached did not profit them, not being mixed with faith in them that heard it. The Word was preached to them, but they didn't release their faith with the Word. The word for agreement is the Greek soon-for-ne-o - it is the English word Symphony it means harmony to be on one accord. So, we must release our faith with reality which is the Word of God.

Once again God is real, but I have to allow Him to be intimate in my life and I must be intimate in His life. It starts with His word and me seeking His kingdom whenever you read the scriptures take it as He is speaking directly to you. Personal is relating to belonging to a single or person rather than to a group or an organization. It is good that your parents, niece, associates, and pastor knows God, but do you know Him for yourself? That is the question that you have the answer too. Psalms 42:1-2 As the deer panteth after the water brooks, so panteth my soul after thee, O God. My soul thirsteth for God for the living God: when shall I come and appear before the living God. When I was young, I believed everything people said I was very naive. This went on for years one day I said to myself if I can believe God the way I believe people God will bless me. After that I started asking God to let me believe Him, the way I believe people but even greater. Some of the reasons we readily believe people is that we can see them. And what we can see, hear, and touch we tend to believe or to believe in it. Initially we were not taught to believe in God or the unseen. 2Corinthians 4:18 While we look not at the things which are seen, but at the things which are not seen: for the things which are seen are temporal; but the things which are not seen are eternal. Blaspheme against the Holy Spirit is a serious offense.

Blaspheme is to speak impiously not showing respect or reverence for someone. Also, to criticize in an abusive or angrily insulting manner. Mark 3:28-29 Verily I say unto you, all sins shall be forgiven unto the sons of men, and blasphemies wherewith soever they shall blaspheme: But he that shall blaspheme against the Holy Spirit hath never forgiveness but is in danger of eternal sin. Matthew 12:31-32 Wherefore I say unto you, all manner of sin and blasphemy shall be forgiven unto men: but the blasphemy against the Holy Spirit shall not be forgiven unto men. And whosoever speaketh a word against the Son of man, whosoever speaketh against the Holy Spirit, it shall not be forgiven him, neither in this world, neither in the world to come. Is it possible to fight against God and not know it? Tradition does it all the time. Matthew 12:22-28 Then was brought unto him one possessed with a demon, blind and dumb: and he healed him, insomuch that the blind and dumb: both spake and saw. And all the people were amazed, and said, Is not this the son of David? But when the pharisees heard it, they said, this fellow doth not cast out demons, but by Beelzebub the prince of the demons. And Jesus knew their thoughts, and said unto them, Every Kingdom divided against itself is brought to desolation; and every city or house divided against itself shall not stand: And if Satan, cast out Satan, he is divided against himself; how shall then his kingdom stand? And if I by Beelzebub cast out demons, by whom do your children cast them out therefore they shall be your judges. But if I cast out demons by the Spirit of God, then the Kingdom is come unto you.

People can be religious and lost John 5:39-42 Search the scriptures; for in them ye think ye have eternal life: and these are they which testify of me. And ye will not come to me, that ye may have life. I received not honour from men. But I know you, that ye have not the love of God in you. Church hurt or denominational hurt Psalms 55:12-14 For it was not an enemy that reproached me; then I could have borne it: neither was it he that hated me that did magnify himself against me; then I would have hid myself from him: But it was thou, a man mine equal, my guide, and mine acquaintance. Someone might say people in churches aren't supposed to hurt one another. That should be the case, but reality says it does happen people are shocked when this occurs. They stop trusting a few or many individuals even thou everyone didn't hurt them. Some folks have been hurt by those that were in different denominations, so they became bitter against the Baptists, Pentecostals Church of God in Christ, and the Assemblies or whoever. Thus, people are angry with denominations and have put forth effort toward others to be mindful of them. I believe charlatans should be exposed and prayed for that truth and righteousness will enter their hearts.

Just because I feel like everyone in a denomination are charlatans doesn't necessarily reign correct. Over the years I notice that out of all the denominations that I have encounter. There will be some out of their organization will think they only have the truth. Not everyone in their group feels that way. At the same time, I have met a few groups that think they are only saved. If you are not with them, you are outside the body of Christ and you don't have hope of Salvation. Even thou they will fight against the Word of God lets, go to the scriptures. Ephesians 2:8 For by grace are ye saved through faith; and not of yourselves: it is the gift of God: Not of works, lest any man should boast. Romans 10:9-13 That if thou shalt confess with the thy mouth the Lord Jesus, and shalt believe in thine heart that God raised him from the dead, thou shalt be saved. For with the heart man believeth unto righteousness; and with the mouth confession is made unto salvation. For the scriptures saith, WHOSOEVER BELIEVETH ON HIM SHALL NOT BE ASHAMED. For there is no difference between the Jew and the Greek: for the same Lord over all is rich unto all that call upon him. For WHOSOEVER SHALL CALL UPON THE NAME OF LORD SHALL BE SAVED. This is what Jesus said in John 10:15-16 As the Father knoweth me, even so know I the Father: and I lay down my life for the sheep. And other sheep I have which are not of this fold: them also I must bring, and they shall hear my voice; and there shall be one-fold and one shepherd.

Jesus was letting Israel know that He had to go to the Gentiles nation to bring them into the fold. That we all we be one in Him that is a blessing to all that receive Him Jesus is the true light. John 1:9-14 That was the true Light, which lighteth every man that cometh into the world. He was in the world, and the world was made by him, and the world knew him not. He came unto his own, and his own received him not. But as many as received him, to them gave he power to become the sons of God even to them that believe on his name: Which were born, not of blood, nor of the will of the flesh, nor of the will of man, but of God. And the word was made flesh. And dwelt among us, (and we beheld his glory, the glory as the only begotten of the Father,) full of grace and truth. 2 Corinthians 5:17 Therefore if any man be in Christ, he is a new creature: old things are passed away; behold, all things are become new. Jesus Christ broke down the middle wall of partition between us. Ephesians 2:12-22 That at that time ye were without Christ, being aliens from the commonwealth of Israel, and strangers from the covenants of promise, having no hope, and without God in the world: But now in Christ Jesus ye who sometimes were far off are made nigh by the blood of Christ. For he is our peace, who hath made both one, and hath broken down the middle wall of partition between; Having abolished in his flesh the enmity, even the law of commandments contained in ordinances; for to make in himself of twain one new man, so making peace; And that he might reconciled both unto God in one body by the stake, having slain the enmity thereby: And came and preached peace to you which were afar off, and to them that were nigh. For through him we were nigh. For through him we both have access by one Spirit unto the Father. Now therefore ye are no more strangers and foreigners, but fellow citizens with the saints, and of the household of God. And are built upon the foundation of the apostles and prophets, Jesus Christ himself being the chief corner stone; In whom all the building fitly framed together groweth unto a holy temple in the Lord. In whom ye also are builded together for a habitation of God through the Spirit. We were engrafted into the body of Jesus Christ. Romans 11:16 -25 For if the first fruit be holy, the lump is also holy: and if the root be holy, so are the branches. And if some be broken off, and thou, being a wild olive tree, wert grafted in among them, and with them partakest of the root and fatness of the olive tree; Boast not against the branches. But if thou boast, thou bearest not the root, but the root thee. Thou wilt say then, the branches were broken off, that I might be grafted in Well because of unbelief, they were broken off, thou standest by faith. Be not high-minded but fear: For if God spared not the natural branches, take heed lest he also spare not thee. Behold therefore the goodness and severity of God: on them which fell, severity; but toward thee, goodness, if thou continue in his goodness: otherwise, thou also shalt be cut off. And they also, if they abide not still in unbelief, shall be grafted in for God is able to graft them in again. For if thou wert cut out of the olive tree which is wild by nature; and wert grafted contrary to nature into a good olive tree: how much more shall these, which be the natural branches, be grafted into their own olive tree? For I would not brethren, that ye should be ignorant of this mystery, lest ye should be wise in your own conceits; that blindness in part is happened to Israel, until the fulness of the Gentiles be come in.

I once shared many scriptures with a guy concerning salvation, I asked him if he understood what they said. He said no I don't understand what you are trying to say, his teaching programmed him to reject anything that didn't agree with his mentality about the

Word. He told me God is only coming back for a certain group of people. And only one hundred and forty-four thousand are going to heaven he must have only read up to Revelation 7 chapter and 8verse and stop.

John said he saw a number no man could number. *Revelation 7: 9-17 After this I beheld, and lo, a great multitude, which no man could number, of all nations, and kindreds, and people, and tongues, stood before the throne, and before the Lamb, clothed with white robes, and palms in their hands; And cried with a loud voice, saying, Salvation to our God which sitteth upon the throne, and unto the Lamb. And all the angels stood round about the throne, and about the elders and the four beasts, and fell before the throne on their faces, and worshipped God. Saying, Amen: Blessing, and glory, and wisdom, and power, and might, be unto our God for ever and ever Amen. And one of the elders answered, saying unto me, what are these which are arrayed in white robes? And whence came they? And I said unto him, Sir, thou knowest. And he said to me, these are they which came out of great tribulation, and have washed their robes, and made them white in the blood of the Lamb. Therefore, are they before the throne of God, and serve him day and night in his temple: and he that sitteth on the throne shall dwell among them. They shall dwell among them. They shall hunger no more, neither thirst anymore; neither shall the sun light on them, nor any heat. For the Lamb which is in the midst of the throne shall feed them and shall lead them unto living fountains of waters: and God shall wipe away all tears from their eyes.*

We all know that God is not a denomination He is a Spirit the Supreme being. *John 4:24 God is a Spirit: and they that worship him must worship him in spirit and in truth.* God wants in His church ekklesia the called-out ones to be ecumenical. Ecumenical several different churches promoting the unity of the faith in Jesus Christ on a whole. There are some denominations that holds their church doctrine over the Word of God.

One guy asked me how many arks Noah build to save his family I said one. He then responded and said Well we are the ark that people must go through to be saved. Well, I don't remember reading that in the bible. One person told me that someone told him you must get the Gospel from a black man to be saved. In all honesty the gospel of Jesus Christ is not black, white, blue, red, or yellow gospel but it is power. Romans1:16 For I am not ashamed of the gospel of Christ for it the power of God unto salvation to everyone that believeth; to the Jew first and to the Greek. Some people you can tell them anything when it comes to the good news of Jesus Christ. They put their faith in a man or woman they say inwardly do all my studying, reading, praying, and meditating. I don't mind and they should give it some mind and attention. Acts 17:11 These were more noble than those in Thessalonica, in that they received the word with all readiness of mind, and searched the scriptures daily, whether those things were so.

Some minsters have spoken ill of other leaders defaming them because they don't believe the same way. If it be possible sit down and talked about it, see can you reason things out in love. Many years ago, I was in a store and a preacher in his seventies was sitting at a table. He had a large black bible in front of him and he said son don't listen to me nor anyone else. He pointed at that bible and said if you listen to any body listen to it because it won't tell you anything wrong. The of Word of God is illuminated Psalms 119: 130 The entrance of thy words giveth light; it giveth understanding unto the simple. Psalms 119:105 Thy word is a lamp unto my feet, and a light unto my path. Our five senses are very important in the natural we don't want to lose one of them. We need our eyes to see and ears to hear our tongue to taste and our nose to smell. When it comes to God your faith will be a very important catalyst. When it comes to asking God for something in Jesus name let your faith say that it is already done. Mark 11:24 Therefore I say unto you, what things soever ye desire, when you pray, believe that ye received them, and ye shall have them. We must believe when we pray for our desired request that we have it before we see it. We also must forgive others before we pray that we will be forgiven. Mark 11:25 And when ye stand praying, forgive if ye have ought against any: that your Father also which is in heaven may forgive you your trespasses. Ephesian 4:26-27 Be ye angry, and sin not: let not the sun go down on your wrath: Neither give place to the devil. The twenty-six verses lets us know you can be angry but don't sin.

It also means straighten out whatever is wrong that darkness or death won't find you in a bad attitude. The twenty seventh verse lets us know don't give room or strength to the devil. Many ministers teach on faith, and they should, I have found out that faith has a partner. Sometime answered prays can literally happen overnight. I have notice others answered prays to manifest in weeks while others in months and others in years. Here is faith partner patience is forbearance, fortitude, longsuffering, endurance. The bible says something about faith and patience. Hebrews 6:12 That ye be not slothful, but followers of them who through faith and patience inherit the promise. I thank God that I teach faith and patience it very important that we have balance. I have heard people say that God is moving too slow, and they were going to help Him out. When we try to help God, we can mess things up with our self-righteousness.

We should learn patience James 1:2-4 My brethren, count it all joy when ye fall into divers' temptations; Knowing this, that the trying of your faith worketh patience. But let patience have her perfect work, that ye may be perfect and entire wanting nothing. Some folks are so impatience until they can't wait on God so they seek the devil out. The devil does not play fair you can't trust him. Mark 8:36-37 For what shall it profit a man, if he shall gain the whole world, and lose his own soul? Or what will a man give in exchange for his soul. The devil will offer you a contract at times people won't read the fine print. If you sat at his supper table, he would charge you for your meal. But it doesn't stop there he will also charge you for the chair, fork, plates, spoon, and the air you breathe. Some walk into the contract with a knowing their eyes are wide open, reading the fine print not considering the outcome.

I have heard some people say that God does not speak to people nor influence them. I am not saying that we can blame everything on the devil, but he has influence people lives. So, if the devil can help persuade individuals the creator of the universe can't speak to His creation. Something is very wrong, and it is not with Him and that is for certain. We have listened to people and ourselves more than we have the Word of God. Jeremiah 33:3 Call unto me, and I will answer thee and shew thee great and mighty things, which thou knowest not. When has God stop speaking to his people? you will have to show me some scriptures. The Holy Spirit is still alive and well and moving as Jesus said He would be in the believers' lives. I truly thank God for Jesus sending the Holy Spirit to not just to be with us but to live in us. The Holy Spirit in us is still our teacher 1 Corinthians 2:9-16 But as it is written, EYE HATH NOT SEEN, NOR EAR HEARD, NEITHER HAVE ENTERED INTO THE HEART OF MAN, THE THINGS WHICH GOD HATH PREPARED FOR THEM THAT LOVE HIM. But God hath revealed them unto us by his Spirit: for the Spirit searcheth all things, yea, the deep things of God. For what man knoweth the things of man, save the spirit of man, which is in him, even so the things of God knoweth no man, but the Spirit of God. Now we have received, not the spirit of the world, but the spirit which is of God; that we might know the things that are freely given to us of God. Which things also we speak, not in the words which man's wisdom teacheth, but which the Holy Spirit teacheth; comparing spiritual things with spiritual. But the natural man receiveth not the things of the Spirit of God: for they are foolishness unto him: neither can he know them, because they are spiritually discerned. But he that is spiritual judgeth all things, yet he himself is judged of no man. For who hath known the mind of God, that he may instruct him? But we have the mind of Christ. I have always admired intelligent people I have found a sense of strength in that for me. I have read about Solomon, Michelangelo, Albert Einstein, Plato, Leonardo da Vinci, and others.

I was blessed to have Freddie Wright as my mentor he was very sagacious, tactful, a man before his time. He had attended Grambling, Howard, and Harvard when I initially met him, I was somewhat dense. Freddie had an awesome vocabulary when he conversed, I said to myself who is he trying to impress. Simply I was a child in my thinking 1Corinthians 14:20 Brethren, be not children in understanding: howbeit in malice be ye children, but in understanding be men. It isn't anything wrong with a child acting like one naturally or spiritually until time and application grows him up. Neither one of us were born an adult we were infants then the process of maturation took place. 1Corinthians 13:11 When I was a child, I spake as a child, I thought as a child: but when I became a man, I put away childish things. We grow naturally by eating natural food normally we start off with milk then we graduate to baby food. Basically, the same principles apply we start off with the milk of the Word then we go to the meat of the Word. Hebrews 5:13-14 For everyone that useth milk is unskillful in the word of righteousness: for he is a babe. But strong meat belongeth to them that are of full age, even those who by reason of use have their senses exercised to discern both good and evil.

Don't ever worry about being the same height and size of someone else spiritually or naturally. You don't have their physique and they do not have yours now that does not stop you from training and working out. Freddie educational physique was profound I once ask him man how in the world did you get so smart. He said curiosity my lad curiosity before I started my own study, he shared with me that Michelangelo painted the Sistine Chapel, and he did the Pieta and David. Freddie could drop a ball and tell you how many seconds it took to hit the floor. Freddie was an author, poet, and a great motivational speaker that God used to help broaden my perceptions in life. Freddie told me that the world was bigger than my surroundings. His favorite scriptures was Matthew 11:17 And saying, We have piped unto you, and ye have not danced; we have mourned unto you, and ye have not lamented. Earthly wisdom appeals to the senses and emotions and at times it is very opinionated. Opinion a view or judgment formed about something, not necessarily based on fact or knowledge not all worldly wisdom is bad. The Spirit of God spoke to me and said that men can intelligently say something about a spiritual matter and sound correct and still be wrong. The spiritual wisdom of God is presented. 1Corinthians 2:1-8 And I, brethren, when I came to you, came not with excellency of speech or of wisdom, declaring unto you the testimony of God. For I determined not to know anything among you, save Jesus Christ, and him impaled. And I was with you in weakness, and in fear, and in much trembling. And my speech and my preaching were not with enticing words of man's wisdom, but in demonstration of the Spirit and of power: That your faith should not stand in the wisdom of men, but in the power of God. Howbeit we speak wisdom among them that are perfect: yet not the wisdom of this world, nor of the princes of this world, that come to nought: But we speak the wisdom of God in a mystery, even the hidden wisdom, which God ordained before the world unto our glory: Which none of the princes of this world knew: for had they known it, they would not have impaled the Lord of Glory. God wisdom surpasses men wisdom by far.

1 Corinthians 1:19-27 For it is written, I WILL, DESTROY THE WISDOM OF THE WISE, AND WILL BRING TO NOTHING THE UNDERSTANDING OF THE PRUDENT. Where is the wise? Where is the scribe? Where is the disputer of this world? Hath not God made foolish the wisdom of this world? For after that in the wisdom of God the world by wisdom knew not God, it pleased God by the foolishness of preaching to save them that believe. For the Jews require a sign, and the Greeks seek after wisdom: But we preach Christ impaled, unto the Jews a stumbling block, and unto the Greeks foolishness: But unto them which are called, both Jews and Greeks, Jesus the power of God, and the wisdom of God. Because the foolishness of God is wiser than men; and the weakness of God is stronger than men. For ye see your calling, brethren, how that not many wise men after the flesh, not many mighty, not many noble, are called: But God hath chosen the foolish things of the world to confound the wise; and God hath chosen the weak things of the world to confound the things which are mighty; And base things of the world, and things which are despised, hath God chosen, yea, and things which are not, to bring to nought things that are: That no flesh should glory in his presence. But of him are ye in Christ Jesus, who of God is made unto us wisdom, and righteousness, and sanctification, and redemption: That, according as it is written, HE

STRANGE FIRE, AUTHENTIC FIRE

THAT GLORIETH LET HIM GLORY IN GOD. Earlier I stated that the gospel of Jesus Christ wasn't a color, nor will it ever be. Many people feel like if there are of a certain ethnicity, they are spiritual or more spiritual than others. We know that is the farthest thing from being the truth. Your relationship with God causes you to be close to him, and not your nationality.

Whatever race and culture you belong to you are important the true God of heaven loves you. John 3:16-17 For God so loved the world, that he gave his only begotten Son, that whosoever believeth in him should not perish, but have everlasting life. For God sent not his Son into the world to condemn the world; but that the world through him might be saved. The hallmark to being a disciple of Jesus Christ is this John 13:35 By this shall all men know that ye are my disciples, if ye have love one to another. 1 John 2:15-17 Love not the world, neither the things that are in the world. If any man loves the world, the love of the Father is not in him. For all that is in the world the lust of the flesh, and the lust of the eyes, and the pride of life, is not of the Father, but is of the world. And the world passeth away, and the lust thereof: but he that doeth the will of God abideth forever.1 John 4:20-21 If a man says, I love God, and hateth his brother, he is a liar: for he that loveth not his brother whom he hath seen, how can he love God whom he hath not seen? And these commandments have we from him, that he who loveth God love his brother also. It is one way to God and that is through His son Jesus Christ. John 14:6 Jesus saith unto him, I am the way, the truth, and the life: no man cometh unto the Father, but by me.

One night I attended church I was bless by what I heard. At the end of the meeting the speaker said that God told her that she didn't need Jesus to get to God You just read what the scripture said about coming to God I don't think He has changed His mind. Some individuals say I receive God in my life, but I won't have anything to do with Jesus. While others say I receive Jesus only and I don't need God. Both people are a heretic, some they may not necessarily mean any harm. Yet they are biblically incorrect and a heretic can teach his (belief system) with scriptures to justify his thoughts. Heresy is dangerous because baby Christians can get a hold of that garbage. Others that have been in the Lord for a while can get a hold of it, that may not be sure. In their faith in the things of God can be easily blown away with every wind of doctrine. Ephesians 4:14-16 That we henceforth be no more children, tossed to and fro, and carried about with every wind of doctrine, by the sleight of men, and cunning craftiness, whereby they lie in wait to deceive; But speaking the truth in love, may grow up into him in all things, which is the head, even Christ: From whom the whole body fitly joined together and compacted by that which every joint supplieth, according to the effectual working in the measure of every part, maketh increase of the body unto the edifying of itself in love. Hersey can easily defeat those who don't study or know what the scriptures says.

When you don't know what the Word says people can tell you anything and you might believe it. God and Jesus always work together. 1 John 5:10-13 He that believeth on the Son of God hath the witness in himself; he that believeth not God hath made him a liar, because he believeth not the record that God gave of his son. And this is the record, that God hath given to us eternal life, and this life is in his son. He that hath the Son hath life; and he that hath not the Son of God hath not life. These things have I written unto you that believe on the name of the Son of God; that ye may know that ye have eternal life, and that ye may believe on the name of the Son of God. Grave sucking is an invitation to the world of familiar spirits. The story of a dead man being raised back to life by Elisha bones is interesting. This was a true miracle from God that He performed, a demonstration of His power. 2 kings 13:21 And it came to pass, as they were burying a man, that, behold, they spied a band of men; and they cast the man into the sepulchre of Elisha he revived, and stood up on his feet. Ecclesiastes 9:5-6 For the living know that they shall die: but the dead know not anything, neither have they any more a reward; for the memory of them is forgotten.

Also, their love, and their hatred, and their envy, is now perished, neither have they any more a portion forever in anything that is done under the sun. Initially I didn't know this lady was a witch, she told me that my father wanted to speak to me. I was happy to know that he had been dead for about twenty years. She instructed me to get a tape recorder take it to his grave place it there turn it on and walk away. When I returned, I will have a message of him I had went by Mrs. Claiborne I told her about it. She let me know that wasn't of God I was about to participate in necromancy and not know it. I now know that ignorance doesn't take strength away from the reality of things. Necromancy is a practice of magic involving communication with evil spirits to get knowledge and information necromancy is forbidden by the bible. Leviticus 19:31 Do not turn to mediums or necromancers; do not seek them out, and so make yourselves unclean by them: I am the Lord your God. Isaiah 8:19 And when they say to you, inquire of the mediums and the necromancers who chirp and mutter, should they inquire of the dead-on behalf of the living? Leviticus 20:6 If a person turns to mediums and necromancers, whoring after them, I will set my face against that person and will cut him off from among his people. Deuteronomy 18:11 Or a charmer or a necromancer or one who inquires of the dead, Familiar Spirits are demons that pretends to be a relatives, associates or animals that comes to deceive you. 2 Chronicles 33:6 And he caused his children to pass through the fire in the valley of the son of Hinnom: also, he observed times, and use enchantments, and used witchcraft, and dealt with a familiar spirit, and with wizards: he wrought much evil in the sight of God to provoke him to anger. 2Kings 23:24 Moreover the worker with familiar spirits, and the wizards, and the images, and the idols, and all the abominations that were spied in the land of Judah and Jerusalem, did Josiah put away, that he might perform the words of the law which were written in the book that Hilkiah the priest found in the house of God. The sticks and the cemetery a person told me her cousin wanted her to give her twenty thousand dollars. She refuse to do so her cousin got angry with her and told her that she would give it up one way or another. This person said her relative got some sticks went to the graveyard and start walking back and forth in it cursing her. She then stated she became very sick, and her food started backing up in her system she had to be admitted to the hospital. She stayed there for a while, when she was released, she said her bill was twenty thousand dollars to the penny. A relative told me that someone we knew used to go to the cemetery to get dirt and put it in their pocket. Before they went to the night club to gamble, this dirt was supposed to give them favor to win.

Some necromancy spells take place in the graveyard grave sucking is a major deception from the devil. Grave sucking is when individuals go to the graves of men and women to draw power from them. By laying on their graves in hope that the anointing of God would enter them. Isaiah 8:19 And when they shall say unto you, seek unto them that have familiar spirits, and unto wizards that peep, and that mutter: should not a people seek unto their God for the living to the dead? The bible has already presented to us the condition of the dead. Ecclesiastes 9:5-6 For the living know that they shall die: but the dead know not anything, neither have they any more a reward; for the memory of them is forgotten. Also, their love, and their hatred, and their envy, is now perished; neither have they any more a portion forever in anything that is done under the sun. Therefore, the body is lifeless there is nothing there to draw from. They don't have a memory nor a reward. The love, hate and envy that once was there no longer exist. The Word of God does prove the anointing of impartation. 2 Kings 2:1-14 And it came to pass, when God would take up Elijah into heaven by a whirlwind, that Elijah went with Elisha from Gilgal. And Elijah said unto Elisha, Tarry here, I pray thee; for God hath sent me to Bethel. And Elisha said unto him, As God liveth, I will not leave thee. So, they went down to Bethel. And the sons of the prophets that were at Bethel came forth to Elisha, and said unto him, knowest thou that God will take away thy master from the thy head today? And he said, As God liveth, and as thy soul liveth, I will not leave thee, so they came to Jericho. And the sons of the prophets that were at Jericho, came to Elisha, and said unto him, Knowest thou that God will take away thy Lord from thy head today? And he answered, Yea I know it; hold ye your peace, And Elijah said unto him, Tarry I pray, here; for God hath sent me to Jordan. And he said As God liveth, and as thy soul liveth, I will not leave thee. and they two went on. And fifty men of the sons of the prophets went, and stood, to view afar off: and they two stood by Jordan. And Elijah took his mantle, and wrapped it together, and smote the waters, and they were divided hither and thither, so they two went over on dry ground. And it came to pass, when they were gone over, that Elijah said unto Elisha, ask what I shall do for thee, before I be taken away from thee, And Elisha said, I pray thee, let a double portion of thy spirit be upon me. And he said, thou hast asked a hard thing: nevertheless, if thou see me when I am taken from thee it shall be so unto thee; but if not, it shall not be so. And it came to pass, as they still went on, and talked, that, behold there appeared a chariot of fire, and horses of fire, and parted them both asunder, and Elijah went up by a whirlwind into heaven. And Elisha saw it, and he cried, My father, my father, the chariot of Israel, and the horsemen thereof. And he saw him no more: and he took hold of his own clothes and rent them in two pieces. He took up also the mantle of Elijah that fell from him, and went back, and stood by the bank of Jordan; And he took the mantle of Elijah that fell from him, and smote the waters, and said, where is the God of Elijah? And they parted hither and thither: and Elisha went over. Paul made a spiritual impartation. Romans1:11-12 For I long to see you, that I may impart unto you, some spiritual gift, to the end ye may be established; That is, that I may be comforted together with you by the mutual faith both of you and me. 1Timothy 4:14 neglect not the gift that is in thee, which was given thee by prophecy, with the laying on of the hands of the presbytery. 2Timothy 1:6 Wherefore I put thee in remembrance that thou stir up the gift of God, which is in thee by the putting on of my hands. Hebrews 6:2 Of the doctrine of baptisms, and of laying on of hands, and of resurrection of the dead, and of eternal judgment. Exodus 29:7 Then you shall take the anointing oil and pour it on his head and anoint him. Exodus 29:29 The holy garments of Aaron shall be for his sons after him, that in them they may be anointed and ordained. 1Samuel 16:3 You shall invite Jesse to the sacrifice, and I will show you what you shall do; and you shall do, and you shall anoint for Me the one whom I designate to you. Samuel anoints David to be king. 1 Samuel 16:1-13 And God said unto Samuel, how long wilt thou mourn for Saul, seeing I have rejected him from reigning over Israel? Fill thine horn with oil, and go, I will send thee to Jesse the Bethlehemite: for I have provided me a king among his sons. And Samuel said, how can I go? If Saul hears it, he will kill me.

STRANGE FIRE, AUTHENTIC FIRE

And God said, take a heifer with thee, and say, I am come to sacrifice to God. And call Jesse to the sacrifice, And I will shew thee what thou shalt do: and thou shalt anoint unto me him whom I name unto thee. And Samuel did that which God spake and came to Bethlehem. And the elders of the town trembled at his coming, and said, Comest thou peaceably? And he said, peaceably: I am come to sacrifice unto God: sanctify yourselves and come with me to the sacrifice. And he sanctified Jesse and his sons and called them to the sacrifice. And it came to pass, when they were come, that he looked on Eliab, and said, Surely God anointed is before him. But God said unto Samuel, look not on his countenance, or on the height of his stature; because I have refused him: for God seeth not as man seeth; for man looketh on the outward appearance, but God looketh on the heart. Then Jesse called Abinadab and made him pass before Samuel, and he said, neither hath God chosen this. Then Jesse made Shammah to pass by. And he said, neither hath God chosen this. Again, Jesse, made seven of his sons to pass before Samuel. And Samuel said unto Jesse, God hath not chosen these. And Samuel said unto Jesse, Are here all thy children? And he said, there remaineth yet the youngest, and behold, he keepeth the sheep. And Samuel said unto Jesse, Send and fetch him: for we will not sit down till he come hither. And he sent, and brought him in. Now he was ruddy, and withal of a beautiful countenance, and goodly to look to. And God said Arise, anoint him: For this is he. Then Samuel took the horn of oil and anointed him in the midst of his brethren; and the Spirit of God came upon David from that day forward. So, Samuel rose up, and went to ramah. Another note on the graveyard and familiar spirits a young man got shot and died. A lady was curious about his death one night she went to the graveyard and dug him up. She asked him did my son kill you a demon spoke to her and said yes. We know it wasn't him that spoke but what gave credence and strength to her was her craft she was a practicing witch. So, either way she was going to receive an answer. It was three people across the seas became lost and couldn't be found. Some people went to the town shaman to get help on their whereabouts he conjures up some spirit. They lead him to these three individuals they were found dead. A supernatural manifestation but not of the Spirit of God. Shaman is a person regarded as having access into the spirit world to channels situations to influence people lives. I heard one person said that their dead relative came back and started breathing in their ear. What purpose would that have served. Some people hear noises and things fall on the floor and say that is just so and so letting us know they are still with us. Demons can play on this because they know you are not going to pray or rebuke a supposeably loved one. People find themselves talking to things and it is not so much as who they are talking to but what they are talking too. Familiar spirits, soothsayer, mediums, shamans, and witchcraft deals with the occult hidden powers, secrets, and knowledge concerning the past, present, and future. A person told me she was talking to a dead person in the funeral home as it laid there the corpse spoke from within itself. Then told her that her family was arguing about a situation. When the lady calls the deceased house that information was correct a relative had confirmed it. It was a demon that revealed that information to that young woman. If we are not careful, we could be operating under a wrong spirit thinking it is the anointing of God.

CHAPTER THREE

IS GOD MOVING?

We were having house service one day and someone's sister was missing, quite naturally she wanted to find her; so, we began praying. An older lady that we all admired was there, who said something I had never heard before; let's send her to where her sister is located. Without thought we sent her spirit to where her sister was. All of a sudden, she goes out under the power of (God, or a god); then I heard the Spirit of God say to me (witchcraft). For a moment, I thought how can this be witchcraft when we are praying to God. All it takes is a half of second for anything to get off track, yet I knew that God was speaking to me. I also knew we were in error, but I didn't know how we got there. I noticed something, after the lady awaken, she was cold as ice. Someone asked, where is your sister? She stated, all I saw were bright lights in a certain area which she described. Two days later she was found, but not where her sister said she was. Just like demons can tell you the truth, they will lie to you as well. At that house we unknowingly helped participate in astral projection. Astral projection or astral travel is a term used in esotericism to describe an intentional out-of-body experience (OBE) that assumes the existence of a soul or consciousness called an "astral body" that is separate from the physical body and capable of traveling outside it through the universe. It is dangerous to go outside of your body when it is not authorized by God. When you are in the Spirit of God you are in the Presence of God. You then have his license for flight if you will. The only way for Isaiah to know about the suffering servant Jesus is that he had to be there spiritually. Isaiah 53:1-12 Who hath believed our report? And to whom is the arm of God revealed? For He shall grow up before Him as a tender plant, and as a root out of a dry ground: He hath no form nor comeliness; and when we shall see Him, there is no beauty that we should desire Him. He is despised and rejected of men; a man acquainted with grief: and we hid as it were our faces from Him; He was despised, and we esteemed Him not. Surely, He hath borne our griefs, and carried our sorrows: yet we did esteem Him stricken, smitten of God, and afflicted. But He was wounded for our transgressions, He was bruised for our iniquities: the chastisement of our peace was upon Him; and with His stripes we are healed. All we like sheep have gone astray; we have turned everyone to his own way; and God hath laid on Him the iniquity of us all. He was oppressed, and He was afflicted, yet He opened not His mouth. He was led as a lamb to the slaughter, and as a sheep before it's shearers is silent, So He opened not His mouth. He was taken from prison and from judgment: and who shall declare His generation? For He was cut off out of the land of the living: for the transgression of my people was He stricken. And He made His grave with the wicked, and with the rich in His death; because He had done no violence, neither was any deceit in His mouth. Yet it pleased God to bruise Him; He hath put Him to grief; when thou shalt make His soul an offering for sin, He shall see His seed, He shall prolong his days, and the pleasure of God shall prosper in His hand. He shall see of the travail of His soul and shall be satisfied: by His knowledge shall my righteous servant justify many; for He shall bear their iniquities. Therefore, will I divide Him a portion with the great, and He shall divide the spoil with the strong; because He hath poured out His soul unto death: and He was numbered with the transgressors; and He bare the sin of many, and made intercession for the transgressors. An individual once walked up to me and shared something that she thought was of God, but when I told her it was of the devil; quickly she responded, all I know is that it works. Some people mistake the things of the devil to be that of God. Those very people at times when the Word of God is being demonstrated under the anointing will call the things of God the devil without hesitation. When I am not familiar with the Spirit of God and His Word, I will be unsure about the manifestation of spiritual activities. Whatever our parents and leaders taught us about the scriptures, that is how we will perceive them. Again, if they don't believe what the Word says they will also teach us not to believe. I was in Monroe Louisiana, at a barber shop when I heard a guy say, I know what the scriptures say; but I am confused because my pastor said something different. This isn't strange or weird, it happens more than you know. We look up to our parents and leaders because we want to believe everything they say and of course they could never be wrong! Only if this was a world of make believe would that be true. We must learn to put God Words over men words. Romans 3:3-4 For what if some did not believe? Shall their unbelief make the faith of God without effect? Certainly not: yea, let God be true, but every man a liar; as it is written, THAT THOU MIGHTEST BE JUSTIFIED IN THY SAYINGS, AND MIGHTEST OVERCOME WHEN THOU ART JUDGED. Hebrews 4:12 For the word of God is quick and powerful, and sharper than any two-edged sword, piercing even to the dividing asunder of soul and spirit, and of the joints and marrow, and is a discerner of the thoughts and intents of the heart. Psalms 119:9 Forever, O God thy word is settled in the heaven. God's Word is settled in heaven; therefore, it should be settled in the earth. Not only in the earth, but also in our earthen vessels. We should pray: Father let your Word be settled in me richly in Jesus Name. The word of God in you performs what it says it does. Psalms 119:130 The entrance of thy words giveth light and understanding unto the simple. As you allow the Word to enter you something happens, light appears, and that light brings understanding which gives clarity. Somethings in life at first will appear to be God and others the devil, but as you get familiar with the Word, clarity will come, and confidence will fill your heart. Jesus said, the words that I speak is spirit and life. John 6:63 It is the spirit that quickeneth; the flesh profiteth nothing: the words that I speak unto you they are spirit, and they are life. Whenever situations occur in your life speak what the Word of God says. Do you know how Jesus defeated the devil in the wilderness? He spoke the Word! For He the word. Matthew 4:1-11 Then was Jesus led up of the Spirit into the wilderness to be tempted of the devil. And when he had fasted forty days and forty nights, he was afterward and hungered. And when the temper came to him, he said, if thou be the Son of God, command that these stones be made bread. But He answered and said, it is written. MAN SHALL NOT LIVE BY BREAD ALONE, BUT BY EVERY WORD THAT PROCEEDETH OUT OF THE MOUTH OF GOD. Then the devil taketh Him up into the holy city, and setteth Him on a pinnacle of the temple, and saith unto Him, if thou be the Son of God, cast thyself down: for it is written, HE SHALL GIVE HIS ANGELS CHARGE CONCERNING THEE: and IN THEIR HANDS THEY SHALL BEAR THEE UP, LEST AT ANY TIME THOU DASH THY FOOT AGAINST A STONE. Jesus said unto him, it is written again, THOU SHALT NOT TEMPT THE LORD THY GOD. Again, the devil taketh Him up into an exceeding high mountain, and sheweth Him all the kingdoms of the world and the glory of them; And saith unto Him, all these things will I give thee, if thou wilt fall and worship me. Then saith Jesus unto him, get thee hence, Satan; for it is written, THOU SHALT WORSHIP THE LORD THY GOD, AND HIM ONLY SHALT THOU SERVE. Then the devil leaveth him and, behold, angels came and ministered unto him. Jesus defeated satin with the Word of God it is very important that we study the scriptures. When we do, we get more familiar with the Word it is important to apply it to your life and other people lives. The Word of God spoken in your life is always a blessing. A logos and a rhema word are always a blessed occurrence. A logos word is God's written thoughts, expressions, ideas, and scriptures. A rhema word is a right now word spoken to you by the Holy Spirit and a living word that fits your situation. I'm reminded of the time I wanted to walk on the town bayou, I fasted and prayed until I was filled with the faith to do so. I went to the bayou in expectation of walking on the water. I looked at the water for a moment while imaging that it was hard. I gently placed one foot on the water and to my surprise it gave. That is when reality set in, I pulled my foot back quickly becoming fearful I went home and went straight to bed. I had read about Peter walking on the water several times, I thought I could do the same. Matthew 14: 22-30 And straightway Jesus constrained His disciples to get into a ship, and to go before Him unto the other side, while He sent the multitude away. And when He had sent the multitude away, He went up into a mountain apart to pray and when the evening was come, He was there alone. But the ship was now in the midst of the sea, tossed with waves: for the wind was contrary. And in the fourth watch of the night Jesus went unto them, walking on the sea. And when the disciples saw Him walking on the sea, they were troubled, saying, it is a spirit: and they cried out for fear. But straightway Jesus spake unto them, saying, be of good cheer; it is I; be not afraid. And Peter answered Him and said, Master, if it be thou, bid me to come unto thee on the water. And He said, Come. And when Peter was come down out of the ship, he walked on the water, to go to Jesus. But when Peter was come down out of the ship, he walked on the water. But when he saw the wind boisterous, he was afraid; and beginning to sink, he cried, saying, Master, save me. I couldn't walk on the water because Jesus didn't tell me to do it. Jesus rhema word to Peter was (COME) and he obeyed it. Now that I think about it what would it have proved if I walked on the water? Nothing. If we're not careful, we'll try to fit someone else's rhema word into our lives and when it doesn't work for us, we get angry and frustrated. I should be listening to what He is saying to me, because then it becomes personal. A guy was driving somewhere and God told him to wait five minutes; however, he was in a hurry so instead of obeying God he decided to pray and that would make everything alright. But God wasn't telling him to pray, He told him to wait five minutes. The guy drove down the street, a car from out of nowhere hit him causing a terrible wreck. He and his wife nearly lost their lives. Now someone might question why God allowed the wreck to happen, but God didn't cause the accident. He warned the guy when he told him to wait five minutes, so his disobedience caused the wreck. If he had obeyed God, he wouldn't have been in that wreck. God told me to move to Monroe, I gave Him some excuses why I couldn't. The strongest one I (thought) was that I live here with my mother, and she needs me. My mother would have been just fine, if I had obeyed God. The excuses I had were really no excuses at all because it carried no weight nor strength with God Almighty. Romans1:20 For the invisible things of him from the creation of the world are clearly seen, being understood by the things that are made, even his eternal power and Majesty; so that they are without excuse. (The written Word becoming a rhema word to the reader). You may have read certain scriptures many times for years, but this time it's like the writing leaps off the page at you, causing your mind to wander, now I know I've read this before, but the difference is this time insight came with it. This is a rhema word being manifested in your life. There was a guy that gave his car away and he got blessed with a better one. Other people started giving their vehicles away thinking the same thing would happen for them, but when it didn't, they were confused. He told them that God instructed him to give away his transportation. It's not always good to do what you see other people doing trying to get blessed. I am not saying that we shouldn't sow seeds or give a donation it is biblical. We know that we can't buy anything from God, but we can plant a seed and believe God for a harvest. Luke 6:38 Give, and it shall be given unto you; good measure, pressed down, and shaken together, and running over, shall men give into your bosom. For with the same measure that ye mete withal it shall be measured to you again. If anyone encourages people to give, he or she should be a giver also. It is good to be a sower especially when you are listening to God on what to offer. God will tell people to give different things, follow the instruction that He gives to you. Your obedience will help you be blessed Isaiah 1:19 If you are willing and obedient, ye shall eat the good of the land. Some folks don't want people to bless others, but they want to be blessed. I remember a guy, who I'll call him Ced, he was persuasive and influential in people lives. Ced came into this wealthy man's life and befriended him. He told him not to bless people because if he did it would only hurt them. He said, they needed to learn to trust God, but if that is true; He too must learn to trust God for his blessings. Ced told him to stop having prayer service at his house, because someone was trying to get his money. It was a spirit of deception, Ced was greedy and money hungry. He planted a seed of doubt in this guy's mind against the people of God and it worked. Proverb 16:28 A froward man soweth strife: and a whisperer separateth chief friends. Evil people will get into other ears and say if it was me, I wouldn't do nothing for him. Let him get it on his own yet they want someone again and again to help them. The difference between a handout and a hand up. A handout is when you are looking for someone to support you. If you are healthy and have a sound mind you should be working. A handout is getting assistance to take care of your personal habits instead of your personal needs. A hand up is when you receive that blessing to be used to benefit your life. It is nothing wrong with receiving from God nor people just use Godly wisdom with it. I remember the times I needed money I prayed, and God would bless me financially. At times I would spend the money on something else now I am angry. All I had to do was used common sense and take care of that which is first. Blessing God kingdoms Paying the bills and splurging to spend money freely with no remorse and very little consequence to your bank account. When you bless the Kingdom of God and pay your bills you can rest better. An example concerning the logos and rhema word. The National safety council and it associate wants you safe on the highway. Therefore, you will see words and symbols on signs that are very beneficial for your driving. You will see forty-five per hour speed limit signs you we see seventy miles per hour speed limit signs. You will see detour signs, yield signs and no merging signs that help manage a correct traffic flow. I will call these signs the word (logos) because they are written out for us. I will call the police officer a rhema word because he is a living being. If you are driving down the street and you see the traffic light on green, it determines that you have the right of way (logos.) Suddenly you see the police officer the rhema word steps in the road and holds his hand up you would stop. The officer directs you to turn right because he sees and know things that you don't know. He has led you from danger without you knowing it. Is God Spirit still moving in the earth realm or not? If so, is the anointing flowing through people today? Let the Word of God speaks for himself He has not been silent. Hebrews 13:8 Jesus Christ the same yesterday, and today, and forever. People say it's talking about the nature of Jesus and not His character or the love of Jesus but not his mannerism. Yet all His attributes are synchronize causing Him to be Who He is. You and I can't divide Jesus Christ we now become a heretic. In the simplest and most innocent way and not even be aware of it. That wouldn't necessarily make people bad just misinformed and again dangerous. Especially if they are prominent or influential in people lives. In some cases when it comes to the scriptures people are wanting to be intellectually astute, and biblically correct at the same it will never work in a million years. In other words the Spirit of Yahweh Word and Spirit supersede men logic and intelligence without a doubt. There have been a couple of pastors I knew that had to preach an intellectual jazzy message to please people in their congregation. Because that's what was expected of them one asked me do you think that I am playing with the people. I quickly responded and said yes if he never would have asked, I would have kept silent about the matter. He told me twice that God was dealing with him about anointing and praying over the people in his church building. James 5:13-15 Is any among you afflicted? Let him pray. Is any merry? Let him sings psalms. Is any sick among you let him call for the elders of the church; and let them pray over him, anointing him with oil in the name of the Lord. And the prayer of faith shall save the sick, and God shall raise him up; and if he has committed sins, they shall be forgiven him. This pastor said when he was young, he went to a Pentecostal church and knew about the Spirit of God moving. From time to time while he was preaching, I use to hear him say when some people get happy some run while others speak in an unknown tongue. He did bring the anointing oil in for a brief moment then took it out, I am not clear on what happen concerning that situation. Jesus said in John 14:12 Verily, verily, I say unto you, He that believeth on me, the works that I do shall he do also; and greater works than these shall he do, because I go unto my Father. Jesus didn't limit these scriptures to a few people in this verse He said (he that believeth on me) the works that I do shall he do, and greater works. That is awesome I don't think Jesus was only saying that to hear himself speak. Many individuals said after the twelve original apostles died there is no need for God to perform miracles through anyone. If you get rid of the apostles and prophets you must take out the evangelists, pastors, and teachers also. Why? Because God is a God of balance and structure and as someone once said that He don't do anything halfway. The five-fold ministry is the hand of the Father in the earth realm. If we start removing fingers from the hand it will become handicap not functioning to its full potential. There are several reasons why God place the five-fold ministry in the body of Christ. Ephesians 4-11:16 And he gave some apostles; and some, prophets; and some, evangelist; and some, pastors and teachers; For the perfecting of the saints, for the work of the ministry, for the edifying of the body of Christ, Till we all come into the unity of faith, and of the knowledge of the Son of God, unto a perfect man, unto the measure of the stature of the fulness of Christ: That we henceforth be no more children, tossed to and fro, and carried about with every wind of doctrine, by the sleight of men, and cunning craftiness, whereby they lie in wait to deceive; But speaking the truth in love, may grow up into him in all things, which is the head, even Christ: From whom the whole body fitly joined together and compacted by that which every joint together and supplieth, according to the effectual working in the measure of every part, maketh increase of the body unto the edifying of itself in love. In the book of 1 Corinthians 12 chapter, it makes mention about nine spiritual gifts that are placed in the body of Jesus Christ by the Holy Spirit. 1Corinthians 12:7-12 But the manifestation of the Spirit is given to every man to profit withal, for to one given by the Spirit the word of wisdom; to another the word of knowledge by the same Spirit. To another faith by, the same Spirit, to another the gifts of healing by the same Spirit; To another the working of miracles; to another prophecy; to another discerning of spirits to other divers' kinds of tongues; to another the interpretation of tongues: But all these worketh that one and the selfsame Spirit, dividing to every man severally as he will. For as the body is one, and hath many members, and all the members of that one body, being many, are one body: so also, is Christ. Some individual feel like God should listen and obey them. The way we think about God and life situations isn't the way He thinks. Isaiah 55:6-9 Seek ye God while he may be found, call ye upon him while he is near: Let the wicked forsake his way, and the unrighteous man his thoughts: and let him return unto God, and he will have mercy upon him; and to our God, for he will abundantly pardon. For my thoughts are not your thoughts, neither are your ways my ways saith God. For as the heaven are higher than the earth, so are my ways, higher than your ways, and my thoughts than your thoughts. What is first in our lives will touch God on a positive note or a negative one. Luke 16:15 And he said unto them, Ye are they which justify yourselves before men; but God knoweth your hearts: for the highly esteemed among men is an abomination in the sight of God. Be careful because pride can cause you to fall. Obadiah 1:2-4 "Behold, I will make you small among the nations; You shall be greatly despised. The pride of your heart has deceived you, you who dwell in the clefts of the rock, whose habitation is high; You who say in your heart, who will bring me down to the ground?' Though you ascend as high as the eagle, and though you set your nest among the stars, from there I will bring you down. "Says the Lord. Proverbs 16:18-19 Pride goes before destruction, And a haughty spirit before a fall. Proverbs 6:16-19 These six things the Lord hates, yes, seven are an abomination to Him: A proud look, A lying tongue, Hands that shed innocent blood. A heart that devises wicked plans, Feet that are swift in running to evil, A false witness who lies, and one who sows discord among brethren. Don't be evil and sow discord among people. James 4:11 Do not speak evil against one another, brothers. Proverbs 6:14 Perversity is in heart, He devises evil continually, He sows discord. Proverbs 17:9 Whoever covers an offense seeks love, but he who repeats a matter separates close friends. Titus 3:2 To Speak evil of no one, to avoid quarreling, to be gentle, and to show perfect courtesy toward all people. A note to the continuationist and cessationists we are family because we are in the body of Jesus Christ. We must never try to defame our brothers and sister as thou we are lawyers. In hope that will give our voice strength and credibility to our jury(congregation.) We then create a friendly fire situation where no one truly win. Friendly fire weapon fire coming from one's own side, especially fire that causes accidental injury or death to one's own forces. This takes place in the spiritual realm seemingly without respect for each others This is not true in every case there are many continuationist and cessationist that are friends as it should be. I want to encourage both readers not to listen to the gospel of Jesus Christ. From a time, frame nor from a denominational point of view nor from church doctrine. Neither should we listen to the Gospel from the philosophy (wisdom) of men. Which offer all the right answers from the intellectual realm but does not minister to the spirit of man. 1Corinthians 2:4-5 And my speech and my preaching were not with persuasive words of human wisdom, but in demonstration of the Spirit and of power, that your faith should not be in the wisdom of men but in the power of God. As much as we put faith in our leaders that preach the Gospel, we should put greater faith in the gospel that they preach. Don't put any limitations and restraints on God because He don't know any. The only ones He knows are the ones that we place on him also take the limitations and restraints off yourself. Even when our pastors share a message with us, we should look into it. Acts 17:11 These were more noble fair minded than those in Thes-sa-lo-ni-ca, in that they received the word with all readiness, and searched the Scriptures daily to find out whether these things were so. If I share a message with you look into it we as leaders should never get angry with people for wanting to know the truth. We should never use our influence with people to take advantage of them in any way. Because reaping days are many times closer than we think. Trust in God look to Jesus and allow the Holy Spirit to direct you!